The Complete Handbook for New Administrative Assistants

Tips and tricks to get and succeed at an Administrative Assistant position

Helen Fletschinger

Copyright © 2016 Helen Scheuerman

All rights reserved.

ISBN-13: 978-1545117477

ISBN-10: 1545117470

ACKNOWLEDGEMENTS

This is my opportunity to thank Carol T. who trusted her instincts and asked me help her edit and publish her first book. Her book led to this, my first book. I want to send a huge "thank you" to my manager, Allan S. He is a great manager and I am very fortunate to be working with and for him.

Thank you to my friend Ann U. She always showed a genuine interest in my ramblings as I thought out loud and read her portions of my early drafts. Ann was always supportive and encouraging. I am so grateful to her for her help with this book and for our 35 years of friendship. I want to send a heartfelt thank you to my four fabulous daughters. Watching them strive and achieve in their chosen careers has given me the confidence to spread my own wings and fulfill my own dreams.

CONTENTS

Introduction	i
Becoming an Administrative Assistant	1
Skills Managers Want and Need	7
The Interview	13
First Day(s) on the Job	20
The "Unwritten" Rules	24
Communication	37
Working with and for Your Manager	42
The "Difficult" Manager	47
Performance Evaluations	53
Promotion Opportunities	56
In Summary	58

INTRODUCTION

This book has been written primarily for anyone considering a job as an Administrative Assistant. While there is information here that might help those who have been in the field for a while, it is primarily for those who are just starting out.

I have tried to cover all the topics you will need to prepare for a job as an assistant as well as the skills you will need once you get hired. The tips and information included have been learned over a 25 year career in the field as well as input from a variety of other assistants, some great managers, and Human Resources experts. This book includes a number of my experiences as a Secretary, Administrative Assistant and Executive Assistant in order to make the information real and not just theoretical.

I hope the information provided here will help you to succeed as an Administrative Assistant!

BECOMING AN ADMINISTRATIVE ASSISTANT

From the outside looking in, the role of an Administrative Assistant is frequently considered an entry-level position with limited opportunities for using one's intelligence and abilities along with limited chances for advancement. Many people who are unfamiliar with the job's qualifications assume that it doesn't require a lot of skills or experience.

In today's high pressure business world, managers and talent acquisition recruiters are looking for intelligent, competent people with computer, communications and organizational skills. They need Assistants who can multitask, perform critical thinking, stay organized, maintain confidentiality, meet deadlines and create well written documents, spreadsheets and presentations.

The role of Assistant is very important in today's business world. Managers have so many demands on their time that they desperately need competent, skilled Assistants who are able to step up and be full members of the manager's team. If you are the kind of person who is able to work both independently and as a team player, be a self starter as well as take direction, who takes pride in their work, enjoys being part of a hard working group and doesn't need to be the decision maker all the time (although you will make decisions as an assistant), this might be a good fit for you.

In a tight job market, you might want to consider a job as an administrative assistant. Frequently (although definitely not always), when companies consider cutting back on personnel, they will lay off the higher paid managers while retaining the competent (but lower paid) assistants. The assistants may then be re-assigned to other managers or given new titles and tasks. In a difficult job market, this can be an important consideration.

One drawback or downside to becoming an administrative assistant is the "glass ceiling." It is difficult but not impossible for administrative assistants to be promoted to management positions. Please check out the chapter on Promotion Opportunities for tips on how to break through and move up the ladder.

How to Find Administrative Assistant Positions. Now that you are interested in becoming an Administrative Assistant, how do you get a job? The good news is that most companies need at least one good assistant and the larger the company, the more assistants they need so there are plenty of opportunities out there for you.

One set of options includes checking a variety of on-line job boards and checking your local newspapers for job fairs for your area. Believe it or not, job fairs are a great option for Administrative Assistant positions and you should go to all you can find. Even when a job fair is being held for a specific field (i.e., medical, sales, etc.), you should go and have plenty of copies of your resume with you. Be sure to hand them out to as many recruiters as possible. Many of them will be glad to take your resume and add it to their collection. Once they get back to their offices and sort through all the resumes they have received, yours will stand out from the crowd and, if the recruiter has an opening, you may have a good chance of getting an interview.

Another approach is to make a list of the companies physically located in your geographic area and check out their websites. Many companies now post their open positions on their websites and make it easy for you to apply on-line. If a company you are interested in doesn't have on-line postings, write a cover letter and mail them your resume. At worst you have just spent the cost of a stamp and some time; at best, you could get a call for an interview. Another part of this approach is check with your friends, relatives and neighbors who work locally and ask about any openings that might be coming up. Word of mouth and personal recommendations still count in this electronic age.

Another search method is to attend job fairs. Don't worry if they advertise for specialties such as medical or sales. Go anyway and take plenty of resumes. Remember, most companies need assistants and there is always the chance that you could be handing your resume to a hiring manager (or two) with an open Administrative Assistant position. I actually tried this method once. I went to two job fairs in one week and received over a dozen follow up calls. I went on four interviews and received two job offers. This may have been a fluke. It was certainly a surprise but it was definitely worth the effort.

If you are not sure about being an administrative assistant or while you are waiting to hear back on your applications, you might want to consider applying at a local temporary staffing agency. They will send you out on short-term assignments which can lead to long term or permanent positions. Some companies prefer to use this temp-to-hire route as a way of vetting someone prior to making a job offer. This is also a great way for you to check out different companies to see if you want to work for them. If you have been out of work for a while, this method has some great advantages. First, you will be employed by the agency and you can update your resume accordingly. Second, managers can now see you actually working which may give you an advantage over the people who are just submitting resumes.

Preparing a resume. There are many good books on resume preparation; you should be able to find several at your local library. There is also a lot of information on the internet. Be sure to check the publication dates for your resources so that you are following the most current advice. Styles change even for resumes. You do not want your resume to be ignored or rejected because it looks out-dated or old-fashioned. Out-of-date formatting can also make you look as though your skills are not current. So please, be sure to use only the most current styles.

Last but not least, please tailor your resume for each application. This can be as simple as rearranging your skills to match the job posting. It can also be more complex if you need/want to add more detail to demonstrate how you can fulfill any special needs listed in the posting. Just be sure to match the correct resume with its job posting; you may want to store each resume on your computer with a file name that matches the job posting. This way, when you are called for an interview, you can easily print the correct resume and have a copy with you. Doing this will help make you look like an impressive, well organized potential employee.

Applying for positions. Please read job postings carefully; many of them contain clues to what the job poster is seeking – what skills they need or require and what they would like. If the job posting uses the word "required" for a particular skill that you don't have, I suggest you only apply for that job if you are very strong in all the other listed areas. Then start learning the required skill so that the hiring manager can see that you are serious about the position and capable of learning the skill. You will also be demonstrating your intelligence and common sense.

If the job posting states "preferred," focus on those skills you do have and include your willingness to learn this skill then start learning the preferred skill, if possible. You will have a much better chance of landing a job if you show that you are both prepared and honest.

SKILLS MANAGERS WANT AND NEED

Job postings often list a bewildering variety of requirements; anything from a "professional demeanor" to "ability to work independently and be a team player" (this really isn't a contradiction of terms). The important things to focus on when reading these postings are to (a) distinguish between what is required and what is preferred; (b) you may already have these skills without realizing it and (c) if you feel you don't have a particular skill, remember lots of other people have learned and so can you.

Computer skills. Today's Administrative Assistant needs to be computer literate – there is no way around this. The basic computer skills most often required include familiarity with the Microsoft Office Suite – Word, Excel, PowerPoint and Outlook. You also need to know how to browse and research the internet – and not just the gaming or shopping sites. As a corollary to this, of course, you should be able to type on a full keyboard – the 2-thumb method used on smart phones doesn't transition well to a full desktop keyboard.

If you need to improve your computer software skills, you have a number of options. If you have not worked with Microsoft Office software, you can take adult education classes at a local community college or at a neighborhood high school. You can also get manuals or how-to books from your local library and practice at home. If you do not have this software on your computer, see if your local library has it loaded on their public computers; if they do, you can practice for free. You can also ask relatives or friends if you can practice on their computers. The important point here is that employers are looking for people with basic to intermediate computer software skills. If possible, try to enhance your skills as much as possible; but remember you do not have to be a top performer; you just have to do reasonably well.

Today, many companies also want their assistants to be familiar with smart phones. If you don't have a smart phone or aren't familiar with its many features, find a friend or family member who can give you a lesson or two or check out your local library or high school to see if they are offering a one day or evening class on how to use a smart phone's many features. It might prove very helpful. One woman I know who was employed by a small home-repair company actually worked three days a week from home and ran the office from her company-provided smart phone. She used it to communicate with co-workers, answer customer calls, schedule appointments and generally run the office.

Organizational skills and attention to detail. These two qualifications appear on many job postings and you will have a better chance of being hired if you can demonstrate these skills.

A basic function of an Administrative Assistant is to keep the manager organized which means that you, the Assistant must also be organized. At first glance, this may seem simple and a no-brainer but you will need to be organized every workday from the time you start until the time you leave.

There are lots of suggestions be for being organized on the job from time management classes to all sorts of desk accessories at various office supply stores and websites. You may find some of these useful but most of them are cosmetic. The fundamentals of being organized are fairly simple. You need to keep all your work up-to-date and you need to know where to find everything including paper and electronic documents.

A corollary to being organized is attention to detail. Another way of saying this is: Accuracy is all-important! It is really worth it to take the time to double check yourself – it takes a lot less time than having to hunt for something because you were in a hurry in the first place. These skills are even more critical if you have multiple managers. You will need to be sure that the correct documents and schedules are going to the appropriate manager.

Each job is different but these skills are critical to all of them. If you are not an organized person, you should start developing some organizational skills. There is a lot of good advice on the internet and how-to books in your local library. Perhaps the best advice is to find a friend or relative who is organized and learn some of their tips and tricks. Practice being organized in every room of your home and in everything you are doing – if you can be organized in your kitchen or bathroom, you can probably be organized in the office also.

Scheduling. As an Assistant, it may be your responsibility to maintain your manager's schedule, book meetings and/or travel arrangements. In an office where you work with multiple managers, scheduling can be a real challenge. One trick to simplify this task is to maintain your own calendar where you keep track of what you need to do for upcoming events. For example, you can schedule recurring reminders for yourself (I use this to order the office coffee supplies every Tuesday for the standard Wednesday delivery). You can also use this to remind yourself to prepare a report for your manager's monthly meeting. This is a great way for you to keep or manager on schedule and both of you organized.

Modern technology has taken a lot of the hassle out of scheduling meetings. In the "good old days" the secretary scheduling a meeting would make up a chart with her manager's availability and then call the secretaries of the invitees and to see if/when they were available and plug them into her chart. Hopefully, all the required attendees would be available for a particular date and time. Then she would invite everyone only to find that several people couldn't attend because the slot was filled during the interim. Maddening to say the least! Today, we have scheduling tools such as Microsoft

Outlook that make scheduling a meeting much quicker and simpler.

Travel arrangements are more complicated as they include travel time before and after the event, booking airlines and hotels, clearing the manager's calendar among a lot of other tasks. If this comes up during an interview, I suggest you ask the recruiter or hiring manager about company policies and guidelines and demonstrate your understanding of the complexities.

Ability to multitask and prioritize. This is where a good assistant can shine. The phones keep ringing, people are interrupting, the meeting starts in 5 minutes AND you calmly present your manager with all the copies of the agenda and handouts he/she had requested; along with a list of attendees and a sign in sheet (which he/she did not request but will need).

The good assistant can stay focused on meeting deadlines while dealing with interruptions and last minute requests. There is no getting around this – there will always be interruptions and distractions. The important point to remember is that you need to meet deadlines. Sometimes this can be daunting but a good manager will appreciate and value your efforts.

While being able to multitask can be a positive, you shouldn't try to do it all the time. It is much more important that you strive for accuracy while meeting deadlines. Multitasking is a skill that needs to be used carefully and as a part of overall performance. After all, the bottom line here is that you need to complete assignments – it's not about how many things you are doing, it's about how much you are getting done correctly and on time.

Additional skills. Many job postings also include additional "soft" skills such as good communication skills, interpersonal skills and customer service. These are often difficult to explain or describe. In order to demonstrate these skills, you might want to think about how you utilized them in previous jobs or life experiences.

This list is a general summary of job skills that were gleaned from a variety of job postings. You should read each posting carefully and then modify your resume accordingly. When responding to job postings your resume needs to be adjusted accordingly; take the time to adjust each response to reflect the order of skills listed in the job postings. Remember, don't lie, but definitely demonstrate. Do your best to demonstrate how you have the skills sought and how you can be an asset to the company.

THE INTERVIEW

Interviews are very individual and specific to the particular job, the interviewer and the interviewee. If you haven't been in the workforce for a while or you haven't changed jobs recently, I suggest you go on-line or go to your local library to research interview techniques; there is a lot of great advice available; just be sure to check publication dates to get the most current information. You might also want to do some practice runs. Ask a friend or relative to play the role of interviewer asking you some tough questions; set a timer or have the "interviewer" time you to add some pressure. Repeat the process with different questions so that you can gain confidence before the real interview. The following are some suggestions that could apply to almost every interview:

Prepare. Look up the company website and learn as much as you can about their business, their industry and any other relevant information. Review the job posting; know exactly what they are looking for so that you can focus on your strengths during the interview to compensate for any weaknesses you may have. (Note: it is somewhat unusual for an applicant to have all the skills listed in a job posting. If you happen to be that unusual person, congratulations!) Jot down a few key words that illustrate how you meet each qualification or skill and study the list. If you do this, you will be much better prepared to answer the interviewer's questions and will appear more professional and organized (all good things). Prepare a short list of questions that you can ask the interviewer. These can be about job expectations, and/or opportunities to work on special projects. This will demonstrate that you are a thoughtful candidate who is willing to grow with the company. Remember, no one is a perfect candidate; the trick is to be the candidate who comes closest to filling the company's wish list.

Dress UP. For an interview I recommend business formal. Shoes (no sneakers or sandals), ties for men, minimal jewelry for women. Look neat and professional. When I interviewed at an employment agency, I noticed another woman interviewing at the same time who wore shorts, sandals and an oversize tee shirt. We were both given a skills test; I took the test seriously while the other candidate was bored and inattentive. I was hired immediately while she received a polite brush-off. Moral of the story: going into an interview looking, sounding and performing like a fully prepared and motivated candidate can definitely improve your chances for getting hired.

Be on time. You might even want to be ten or fifteen minutes early in case you need to complete some paperwork. This sounds obvious but I have seen people actually be as much as an hour late for an interview – the recruiter took the next applicant -the person who was late lost out. If, for some reason, you will be unavoidably late (i.e., a major traffic accident) use your cell phone to call the recruiter or hiring manager and let them know. The same applies if you need to reschedule due to an emergency. Recruiters and hiring managers will appreciate your courtesy and professionalism and will usually reschedule the interview

<u>Turn your cell phone off BEFORE you go into the building</u>. Don't wait until the last minute; chances are you will be so stressed you will forget to take care of this ahead of time. You really don't want to be interrupted while you are telling the recruiter or hiring manager how competent you are. I have heard a number of recruiters say that just hearing a candidate's phone is an immediate disqualifier. Turning off your phone before you enter the building is a sure way to avoid this major problem.

<u>Listen carefully</u>. Pay attention to the interviewer and answer the questions he/she asks. This seems obvious, but it can be very hard if you are nervous, anxious and/or stressed. Keep your answers focused just to the question; do not ramble or go off topic. If you do find yourself talking too long, offer a short apology and stop; recruiters and hiring managers usually understand that you may be nervous; just take a deep breath and try to stay more on topic for the next questions.

If you are asked an open ended question such as "describe a project you managed" it is important to include some details about difficulties you overcame and how well you accomplished the task. Again, try to stay on topic, don't ramble and don't go into a flood of detail. Try to keep your answer interesting, informative and to the point (here is where practice beforehand can bring you closer to perfect). If you are unsure about how to manage this part of the interview, you can go on-line and look up the latest trends in interview techniques and questions. You should also write out short paragraphs summarizing a few different incidents and events in career where you were successful and one or two where you could have been better (include how you have improved since then). Read these paragraphs over several times before going to an interview to be sure you are familiar and comfortable with them. This way, you will be prepared and won't have to spend precious moments trying to come up with an answer.

Try to stay calm and remember to breathe! Stay focused on the interviewer. Show that you are interested and can handle pressure. Try to take a deep breath BEFORE speaking. This gives you a moment to calm down and think. You want to be sure to answer the question correctly and professionally.

While an interview may feel like life or death, most of the time, it isn't. Try to keep the interview in proportion – this is for a job, even if it is a dream job. In other words, this is a conversation between you and one or two other people about what skills they are seeking and what ones you have. If you have done your research and have the skills, the more relaxed you are the better off you will be.

Above all, stay honest. You may be tempted to exaggerate your skills or lie about your weaknesses – don't. If you are not qualified for the job, it is better to not start than to be horribly stressed or fired. There are other jobs that could be a better fit for you. As an example: a young woman I know applied for a position where the recruiter felt she wasn't really qualified. However, because this young woman was honest about her skills, a week later the recruiter called her for another position within the company. She took the offer and did very well in the new position and was eventually promoted to her dream job. If she hadn't been honest, she wouldn't be doing so well today.

Skills testing. Most large companies (and even mid-sized ones) now do skills testing. You may be put in front of a computer and given tests in one or more software packages. I recommend that you practice your skills before you go for the interview. You can borrow some software manuals from the library and go through them to refresh your memory about tips and tricks you've forgotten and learn a few new ones. Before and during the test, remember to breathe and think! Take a moment or two to read and then re-read the question. This will give you time to think; you will probably know many or most of the answers – just give yourself time to think of them. You don't want to have a great interview only to lose the job because you forgot how to do a particular type of formula or format a table

Remember to thank people. Be sure to thank the interviewer and the receptionist as you are leaving the interview. When you get home, send the recruiter a thank you email or note after the interview. If you don't hear from the company within a week, send a very polite, non-pushy follow up email. Courtesy means a lot in today's business environment. If you are on the short list for a position, courtesy and a pleasant manner could be the dealmaker. If you don't get the original job, your courtesy and follow through might help you get the next opening. I cannot stress enough how important it is to both competent AND courteous, the two go together very closely to make a great candidate and employee.

Follow up interviews. Some companies may call you back for multiple interviews; this is more likely to happen in larger companies where recruiters do the initial screening and then schedule the best applicants to meet with the hiring manager/s. If you find yourself in this position, you should make a point of being on time and following all the points above for each interview. It would be very sad if you survived two or three interviews only to be late or have your cell phone go off during the last one. Treat each follow up interview as if it were the most important. On the other hand, remember that you might not be the only applicant being called for a follow up so don't blame yourself if you don't make it to hiring; just do your best each time.

FIRST DAY(S) ON THE JOB

Congratulations! You have been hired and you are now an Administrative Assistant. What do you do now? Of course, each job is unique in the details but most jobs have a number of basic points in common. Here are some suggestions that should help smooth your adjustment:

Be on time. It will make a very bad first impression if you are late or even if you are too early (showing up at 6:00 am for a 9:00 start is a bit extreme). If you are unsure of how to get to your new job, plan out the route ahead of time and leave an adequate amount of time to compensate for rush hour traffic. If you have an emergency that will make you late or miss the first day, call your new manager as soon as possible; if you don't have his/her phone number, contact your recruiter. After all, emergencies happen, just be sure to let people know – they should be understanding but only if you let them know.

Dress appropriately. Consider wearing the same type of outfit and accessories you wore to the interview. It worked there so it should work for your first day. During the day, look around and see how your manager and the other employees are dressed to get a feel for how you should dress going forward. A good tip is to dress more like your manager, especially if you want to eventually work toward a promotion. If your new co-workers look too dressed down or up, check to see if this is due to a special event such as an inspection or celebration.

Introductions. As you are introduced to the people in your office, do your best to remember as many names, titles and faces as possible. Unless it is a small office, you will have to keep working at this until you are familiar with all of them. This may seem very obvious; however, it will help you avoid making some serious social/business mistakes. You don't want to ignore a request from a senior manager simply because you didn't recognize his or her name.

Pay attention. Listen to the information you receive at your orientation. Don't hesitate to ask questions if you need clarification or more information. You need to know about your start and end times, lunch and coffee breaks, how the phones should be answered, and many other details. If you aren't given a formal orientation, it is even more important to ask questions. You also want to be sure you understand the answers; if you are not sure, ask!

Be forewarned and avoid this mistake! Sometimes a long orientation can be boring with many speakers and slide presentations, the room is warm, you did not sleep the night before and you may start to feel drowsy. No matter how boring the speaker is, you do not want fall asleep, get caught and lose your job before you even start. Also, dress appropriately for orientation; again, this seems obvious but a recruiter friend of mine complains of people showing up in shorts and sandals for orientation. They get turned away and lose out on some great jobs.

Company policies. Ask if there is a company policy and procedure manual and/or an employee handbook. If there are, learn where they are located and read them. Knowing what the company considers acceptable and unacceptable will help you avoid unnecessary mistakes. These handbooks and manuals contain a wealth of information that you will find useful – they can cover everything from dress codes to special benefits such as marriage leave to retirement plans.

Job description. Most mid-sized and large companies have job descriptions (they may have different names but serve the same function). Job descriptions usually list all the standardized functions for a generic position such as "Administrative Assistant." However, a generic job description will probably not include the special or unique functions and skills required for a specific department within the company. For instance, you may get a job where you are making a lot of travel arrangements for your manager who travels constantly for business. These skills may not be listed in your generic job description but they are certainly part of your job. So be prepared for the unexpected assignments. By the way, I have found these surprise tasks are usually the most interesting and rewarding ones.

Even if you are given a job description, you should ask about your specific duties and responsibilities. If possible, ask the person who is hiring you, before you start work. Otherwise, ask your new manager as soon as possible after you start work. Be sure to write down the list of duties! This way you will know what to expect and be better prepared to handle the surprises.

In conclusion, the most interesting line of most job descriptions is frequently the last line which translates to "and any anything else your manager(s) can dream up." Be prepared. At various times in my career I have found myself: teaching computer software skills at my company's corporate university; assisting with payroll; maintaining the photocopiers and serving as recording secretary on a committee that was revising the company-wide policy and procedure manual. Most of these assignments were interesting, some were fun, others were educational and all of them helped me grow and learn.

THE "UNWRITTEN" RULES

In any office, there are unwritten rules of behavior. Following these rules can help make your time on the job a more pleasant and less stressful; failing to follow these rules can sometimes cause stress, embarrassment and even cost a promotion, a raise or even your job. Most of these rules will seem obvious and good old-fashioned common sense; however, a gentle reminder once in a while just might be useful.

Courtesy. Good manners, such as saying "good morning" and "thank you," go a long way in the business world. Taking the time to smile and pay a sincere compliment can make a co-worker's day and have huge benefits for you later on. The most important point here is to be sincere – people catch on very quickly to the phony or insincere and they don't like it – and have some painful ways of showing it.

Being courteous also entails being a good listener if someone is having a bad day; and (very important) not repeating what that person said. It means showing respect for everyone around you no matter his or her position in the company. Remember, the person you are talking to just might be related to a senior manager or be the person who will have input into your next raise or promotion. On a personal note, I had been courteous and helpful to someone who worked in another department. Years later, when an interesting position opened up in his department, he offered it to me; I was delighted to accept as I knew it to be a very interesting and rewarding one.

I strongly recommend being nice to those around you, smiling when you speak to them, having a pleasant word for others, from the housekeeping team to senior management. At the very least, this will make you feel good and make your day go faster. Additionally, those around you will be glad to have you around which is always nice. Third, it will win you friends who will be able to assist you when you need help. Finally, your reputation as a competent professional who is pleasant, cheerful and willing to assist others should help you if/when you are seeking a promotion or raise. So keep smiling.

Accuracy and proofreading. Accuracy and proofreading are critical. This applies to documents, spreadsheets, presentations, emails and anything else you might work on. The best way to ensure accuracy is to, first, be careful what you are typing and, second, to go back and carefully double check and proofread.

When working on documents and emails, do NOT rely on the automated spell checking. The software does not know if you mean "form" or "from" which have very different meanings. This is only one of thousands of examples of how a spell-checking feature can ruin a perfectly good document; you need to use your eyes and pay attention to the details. Just remember all the sloppy emails and solicitation letters you have laughed about; you really don't want your email or document to be the next office joke.

Spreadsheets demand a different level of accuracy and proofreading in that you need to test your formulas. What may look correct at first or second review could, in fact, be hiding a serious error which can create havoc when you least expect it. For example, I had a spreadsheet with date formulas that looked correct. I tested the formula by adding dates – it worked. Then I tried subtracting and found the error. I can only say – test, test and test again (and don't use the same type of test each time). In the final analysis, it is much, much better to take an extra five minutes to proofread and test for accuracy than have to spend more time listening to your manager while trying to correct the errors.

Filing is another area where accuracy is important. You always want to double check to be sure you are putting the correct piece of paper in the correct file. If you are working in a "paperless office" you should be equally careful to create directories and subdirectories or folders that are clearly and accurately labeled and that you use equal care to save documents to the correct folders.

Timeliness. There are two aspects to timeliness: being on time to work and meeting deadlines. Both of these may seem self-evident;

however, each one consistently has been a top manager complaint for years.

While managers understand that we might be late for work occasionally due to traffic or transit delays, family issues, etc., they get very annoyed with staff members who are frequently late. Managers are, therefore, more likely to reward staff members who are consistently on time or early. If you find that you are running late, call or send a text message to your manager and include a the reason and a realistic estimate of when you hope to make it into the office – he/she will appreciate your professionalism.

If you are someone who has a hard time getting to work on time, develop some skills to keep yourself on track. If you find you have a hard time getting up or out on time, try setting your alarm 15 to 30 minutes earlier; I used this trick and so that I could take my time waking up before I had to start moving. You can also look at your morning routine to see if you can change some things to ensure you get out early enough arrive at work on time. For instance, if you prepare your lunch in the morning, try preparing it the evening before.

Meeting deadlines can sometimes be a major challenge, even for the best of us. The report has to be finished by 2:00 pm, and it is now 11:00 am – 3 hours, easy, right? Wrong. The phones start ringing, three people need your assistance (each one has a different request), your manager just got a call from the Vice President who needs a document immediately (of course, it is an old, archived one). Suddenly, you have 40 minutes instead of 3 hours – where did the time go??? If you are faced with this type of problem, let your manager know as soon as possible. He/she can then hold non-critical work until you are done; your manager can also inform others in the office that you not to be disturbed as you are on a deadline. This has worked well for me, especially when I was working on something important to a senior manager. Finally, if you need help, ask for it. After all, you are part of a team. See if someone else can answer the phones for a while or take care of some of the special requests. Just don't procrastinate.

My advice for this is to develop the habit of starting projects as soon as possible after they are assigned. Don't wait. Never assume you will have enough time later – you won't. It doesn't matter the size of the company, the number of managers or the number of assistants, there will always be interruptions. Try using a calendar (I use an on-line calendar) and post reminders ahead of your due dates and milestones. When I have a lot of tasks and projects, I rely on a to-do list. One of my co-workers uses Post-It notes, one for each task. She arranges them in columns and rows and removes them as they are done and re-arranges the remaining ones as priorities change. As I said above, find what works for you just don't procrastinate.

Flexibility. This is a skill that almost everyone needs in the workplace. This skill has become even more necessary in today's open concept offices and cubicles without doors. A part of flexibility is knowing when to allow the distraction and when to remain focused on the task in hand.

The main "interrupter" is usually the phone. You are typing away, keeping on deadline when the phone rings. The caller could be a senior manager with a time consuming request that needs immediate attention, a disgruntled customer or a bored co-worker. No matter who the caller is or their issue, first you should always remain courteous. Next, prioritize the caller and their request; for instance, can you delay your deadline, can you transfer the caller to someone else, or should you notify your manager of the caller and their issue? Bottom line – don't lose sight of the caller and their issue; make sure that it will get the proper attention while, at the same time, you make sure that you meet your deadline. If you can't do both, ask for help; let your manager know what happened or ask a co-worker for assistance. A big part of flexibility is being able to unbend enough to ask for help when you need it.

When you find yourself at the mercy of a co-worker like the office "chatterbox" you might want to use a trick that I found helpful. When cornered by someone who wanted to talk and talk and talk, I wait until s/he is just ending a "verbal paragraph" and then quietly say "I'd like to hear the rest of this but I have to get this work done for a deadline." This way, there are no hard feelings and you can get back to work.

Remember, interruptions will happen – you need to learn to deal with them and move on. Stressing over these distractions doesn't help solve the problems. Building in extra time to meet important deadlines and asking for help when needed will usually be much more effective.

Teamwork. The first point to consider is: Who are your team members? And yes, this is a trick question. It actually depends on the task or project you are working on at the moment. At any given time, your team could include you and: your manager, the other assistants in your department, your counterparts in the building, department members in another state or country, consultants, an approved vendor, and/or your company's clients along with their staff. Essentially, it is you and anyone you are working with, working for and/or managing.

The next point to consider is how to build and maintain teamwork. If you are new to a company or department, you should make a point of introducing yourself to the people around you. Then keep your ears open, listen and learn how they conduct both official and unofficial business. Be courteous and ask for assistance and clarification if (when) you are in doubt about how something should be done. Keep working at this and sooner or later, you should become accepted as part of this team.

When it comes to people outside your immediate area, follow the same procedures as above – introduce yourself in emails or over the phone as opportunities arise; don't be aggressive or pushy but definitely polite, helpful and outgoing. These contacts do pay off. As you become comfortable and you become a member of different teams, be sure to participate fully. Don't sit back and let everyone else do the work – you will need to pitch in and do your fair share (and maybe a little more) of the work. If you don't, you will find that the others will not be willing to help you when you need their assistance. I cannot stress or repeat this enough – teamwork is vital for the success of anyone in business and that includes Assistants.

Networking. Networking is more fluid and less structured than teamwork. It is more about building useful contacts with people both inside and outside your company. Anyone can be a networking contact so you should always be putting "your best foot forward." A vendor, customer, co-worker or senior official could easily become a networking contact.

If you work for a mid-sized or large company, make a point of getting to know people in the other departments and divisions. When you have a large project or are applying for a transfer, these contacts can prove useful. In conclusion, you want people to remember you as a positive networking contact and not someone to avoid. You should always strive to be competent, courteous, and capable.

Confidentiality. This is a critical aspect of many, including Administrative Assistant positions in today's information age. The higher your manager's position, the more important this becomes as you could be privy to all types of information from personnel disciplinary information to insider trading information. If you are hired for a position in the healthcare field, you could also be privy to patient information. Be aware that most confidential information is actually protected – in some cases by company policy and in other cases, such as patient information, by federal law. Failure to protect this information could get you fired or even convicted of a felony so please be careful. If someone asks you for information or even a hint, remember that you could face some serious consequences. Do not even offer a hint or suggestion as this is a slippery slope; once you start it is hard to stop and sooner or later you could find yourself in a black hole with no way out. Here are a few suggestions you can say for handling this type of situation: "I don't recall;" "I am not sure;" or "I'm sorry, that information is confidential." Just do not give out confidential information.

Office Gossip. This topic might seem like fun and a great way to bond with your co-workers. But remember if you are in a group (or even another individual) gossiping about someone down the hall today, that group or person could easily be gossiping about you tomorrow. Another point to remember about gossip is that the person you are sharing a juicy item with might turn out to be the relative, friend or close co-worker of the person you are discussing – this can at best be embarrassing and at worst cost you a raise, promotion or even your job.

If you find yourself in a group that starts gossiping leave quietly if possible. If not possible, try to change the subject or stay in the background. Do not add to the conversation and never repeat it. I have been an assistant over more than two decades and have seen the damage and pain gossip can cause; believe me, it is not worth it. By the way, one of my personal observations on the subject of "gossip" is that gossipers rarely (if ever) get the facts right.

Office Romance. This is a very tricky and touchy subject but it really needs to be considered. The all-important point here is: many people love a romance and they also love to gossip about it. Therefore, if you do find yourself romantically involved with someone in your office – keep it OUT of the office and away from the gossipers, especially if one or both of you happen to be married.

I realize that you might be so happy that you will be tempted to share your good news. That's fine – you can share with your friends and family; just do not share it with anyone in your company. Yes, I typed "company". If you share with someone in another department or building, the news will get back to your department/office – gossip is probably the fastest moving commodity in any company or civilization.

I am not going to say "don't get involved with anyone in your office or company" primarily because I did. I met an amazing man in my company (from a different department) and we had many wonderful years together as a couple. Fortunately, we did not work together often and were spared most of the gossip. However, over the years, I have heard many stories about other people. Most of the gossip was disparaging and some was downright ugly. I can only repeat what I said above: keep your personal relationships OUT of the office. End of lecture (but with my best wishes).

Dress for Success. Choosing what to wear at the office can be extremely challenging. Different parts of the country, different ethnic groups, different genders and even different age groups all have distinctive opinions about what is and is not acceptable. So what should you wear?

For the first day, I suggest you consider wearing the same type of clothes that you wore for your interview – if it got you the job, it should be at least moderately appropriate. Once you start working, review the company's policy and procedure manual (if the company has one) for an official dress code. Take the time to observe how formally or casually your manager dresses. As their assistant, you should consider following his/her lead. If there are other assistants in your work area, check out how they dress; but be careful – you only want to emulate the "good" assistants who are getting the better assignments and positive recognition. Also, follow the lead of your better dressed and groomed co-workers, you want to be seen as one of the up and comers rather.

If you are working towards a promotion, I suggest you follow the dress code for the new position; it may not get you the promotion but not doing so could have negative consequences. If you like where you are but want a salary increase, dress like you deserve it. Remember, for promotions and raises, the quality of your work is very important but following some subtle or unwritten rules can frequently be a big help.

The following are some "don'ts" or "limits". This list was compiled not only from years of observation but also from working in a corporate Human Resources department and being part of a team that actually wrote these rules for our company.

- Jewelry – go easy on the jewelry, it can get in the way and be a distraction. I know of one woman who nearly got her long necklace caught in a shredder – only her quick reaction averted a disaster.

- ✥ Perfume, etc. – limit the amount of scent you use. Whether it is after-shave, perfume, etc. Not only is it a distraction but some of the people around you may be allergic. Please be considerate of your co-workers and any visitors to your office.

Dress for the office – remember this is an office, not a nightclub or a dating service. Avoid clothes that are too tight or provocative (this goes for both men and women). Also observe how people are being treated – the ones wearing tight or inappropriate clothes may get attention but are they getting the good assignments, raises or promotions?

The important point of this section is for you to be aware that companies and departments have many "unwritten" rules. Some of these are definitely job related and others can be considered "business/social." Especially during your first days on the new job interact with your co-workers slowly and courteously. Get to know how things are done and see how people interact. Then emulate the ones who are treated with respect (especially by the managers). You want be noticed for the quality of your work and you ability to a positive member of the team.

COMMUNICATION

There are, of course, many ways to communicate in the office; and just as many ways for us to put our feet into our mouths up to our eyebrows. Therefore, my first ten rules for communicating can be summed up as "think first." Do I follow these ten rules? All I can say is that I try hard to follow my own advice and I hope that you can do even better.

Phones. We all know how to use phones, right? Probably. We all know how to speak on the phone, right? Wrong. How many phone calls have you had where the other person mumbles; or speaks too fast, or too loud or too soft; or constantly interrupts; or doesn't let you get a word in? The best (and shortest) tip I can give you is: Recall all the things you hate to hear in a phone conversation and don't do any of them. In other words, during phone calls and when leaving voice messages speak clearly, repeat phone numbers (especially when leaving voice messages), check to make sure the person on the other end of the conversation has all the information s/he needs and repeat any information you receive to verify accuracy. Getting a message right the first time can save a lot of hassles in the long run.

In the current business environment of open offices and cubicles, you want to be aware of how your voice carries. Just as you may not want to listen in on your co-workers' conversations, remember that you may not want them listening in to yours.

As an assistant, you will probably have to answer a lot of phone calls and take a lot of messages. You should answer the phone every time as if the caller is the company CEO or your manager's best customer. This way, when they do call, you are prepared and everyone else will value your competence.

When you take messages, your manager will be grateful if you write clearly. More to the point, he/she will also appreciate it when you include all pertinent information including name, phone number, time of call, and reason for call. My manager still teases me about the time I left off the last digit of an important phone number; I haven't made that mistake again.

Emails. Emails have become a major form of communication in the business world but there are still a lot of people who don't seem to know (or choose to ignore) the basic rules for emails. To help you navigate this thorny topic, here are some email dos and don'ts:

- **Privacy** - there is absolutely, positively no such thing as a "private" email. Privacy with regard to emails is in the same category as unicorns and little green men from Mars. Never put anything into an email that would embarrass you if the email were forwarded to your manager, the CEO, your company's legal department, or your family. Once you send an email, it is completely out of your control and the recipient(s) can send that email to anyone, anywhere, at any time (even years later when you are about to get promoted).

- **All capitals in an email** – NEVER do this! This is the written equivalent of "screaming, ranting, and raving". It is also considered a major insult. On the other hand, if you receive an email with all caps – please read it first. It could just be someone who did not know the rules wishing you a happy birthday or "have a nice day". If you find yourself working with, or emailing with, someone who doesn't seem to know this rule, you may want to share this tip. It could help him/her avoid some major misunderstandings.

- **Proofreading** – After you type any email, stop and read it BEFORE you send it and correct any grammar or spelling errors. As I mentioned earlier in this book, do not rely solely on your software's spell check feature – you have probably had a good laugh over emails where people have obviously failed to follow this rule with unfortunate results. After all, you want to people to think of you as intelligent and competent; a sloppy email can seriously undermine that impression. So proofread your emails before you send them – you cannot undo them once they are out there.

- **Upsetting emails** – you will occasionally get an email that leaves you upset or angry. Be very careful how you respond. Remember the bullet point above regarding privacy. If necessary, go ahead and type a vehement response. Just leave the recipient lines blank and do NOT send it. Walk away and cool off, first. Then go back, re-read your response and edit it in light of the first bullet point above. Be aware of the worst case scenario: the recipient of your irate email could try to use your response to make you like the bad guy. Try to practice the advice I received when I was young: "Do not stoop to the other person's level, try to bring that person up to yours". I have found this to be very good, practical advice when it comes to emails.

- **Recalling emails** – Some email packages let you "recall" your emails if they are "unread." What they do not tell you is that recipients can (and very frequently do) preview their emails in a "reading pane." The recalled email could look like it was unread but, in reality, the recipient could have already read it. So be careful – as an old proverb states: "An ounce of prevention is worth a pound of cure."

It is always important for us to think before we speak and this applies to both our personal lives and our business ones. It is so easy to say the wrong thing and usually impossible to undo the damage afterward. So be careful of what you way and write. The wrong word can cost you a promotion, a raise or even your job. On the other hand, the right, thoughtful or courteous word can earn you that promotion or raise. So, please, think before you speak or write.

WORKING WITH AND FOR YOUR MANAGER(S)

While your manager is your boss, you and your manager are team members. As you settle into your new job, you should strive to create an atmosphere where you both work well together. Ideally you and your manager should eventually learn the way you each think and work and the teamwork should become smoother and smoother. The closer and better you and your manager work together, the smoother and better your department or company will run and the more successful you will both be. This may seem obvious but I have seen too many people treat this position as just another job. They didn't put in the effort to make or build a team with their manager and eventually they lost out; when their manager either left for another job or was promoted they did not take their assistant with them and the assistant was let go. On the other hand, I also know of several assistants who did a great job supporting their managers; when their managers left (some retired, another was fired) the assistants were retained and given special assignments until new managers were hired. In the end, it usually pays to be a supportive, team player.

Support Your Manager. In previous sections, I covered many of the duties and tasks an Administrative Assistant may be required to perform; however, no two jobs are exactly alike. One way to ensure that you are performing your specific job well is to ask your manager what s/he wants and expects from you as their assistant – what skills and work qualities is s/he looking for and where can you improve. Then work to meet these expectations. For instance, your manager may be very concerned about customer service, meeting deadlines, taking detailed messages, and/or other skill(s). The more you know about your manager's priorities and preferences, the easier it is to fulfill them. Additionally, as you and your manager build a team, you should pay attention to areas where you can provide additional support. For instance if your manager is frequently late for meetings, you can suggest some options for how you can assist him/her such as building in time cushions between meetings or sending text message reminders.

Another important aspect of the assistant's role is to ensure that your manager always "looks good" to his/her boss, other managers and to your company's and department's clients (such as in-house staff, outside clients and vendors). This includes: making sure that all reports are accurately completed in a timely manner; all messages are delivered promptly and all documents needed for meetings are available ahead of time. Remember, when your manager looks good, you look good. When he/she doesn't look good, you look bad.

It is also important to own your mistakes. If you miss a deadline or forget to tell your manager about a phone call, or find a typo in an important document, admit it to your manager promptly, own your mistake and try not to make the same mistake again. Your manager should respect and appreciate your honesty and maturity. After all, none of us are perfect.

Working for and with Multiple Managers. In today's job market, it frequently happens that an Administrative Assistant will be assigned to multiple managers which can give new meaning to the term "multi-tasking." This type of position can involve overlapping deadlines, dueling egos, scheduling conflicts and serious headaches. On the other hand, it can also be challenging, rewarding and stimulating. So, if you are up for a challenge and are able to juggle multiple schedules, this could be a good fit for you.

Prioritizing the workflow for multiple managers is an important key to success. Each manager has their own deadlines and each deadline is important. If one manager is senior to the others, prioritizing becomes (a little) simpler; if they are all equal, it is more challenging. A typical problem relates to deadlines. For instance, you may have two (or more) managers who need their reports done by 2:00 pm, if you can meet both deadlines successfully, great! If not, let the managers know as early as possible about the conflict as soon as possible so that they can negotiate the priorities. Please don't wait until 1:55 to let them know – you will only cause more problems by waiting. By letting all the managers involved know in advance that you will have a conflict, they should be able to negotiate a solution for you – by changing one or more deadlines, getting you some help or relieving you of other duties such as answering phones. Remember, they cannot help you solve the problem unless they know it exists.

When working for multiple managers, you really and truly must learn to speak up about any conflicts or overlaps – this is probably the most important part of this type of job! You and all your managers are part of one team –it is critical that you be open and honest about your job issues with them. Face it - if you don't communicate with them about work and scheduling conflicts, they will assume that everything is going smoothly. When you finally drop the ball (and you will if you don't speak up), all your managers will be justifiably angry. Also, you will become overwhelmed and it is certain that you will get burnt out very quickly.

One suggestion for staying organized is to keep your own detailed calendar of upcoming deadlines including all your managers' upcoming events and potential deadlines. This way, you will be able to go to a manager and remind him, well in advance, of an upcoming event and suggest you start preparing documents well before deadline to avoid conflicts and last minute interruptions. Most managers will appreciate your reminders and value your organizational skills. Even if you have one or more procrastinators among the managers, at least you will be able to lessen the last-minute stresses.

It is important to stay organized and speak up. Your managers need to be aware of the challenges and problems of sharing an assistant and it is up to you to keep them informed of conflicts while, at the same time, meeting all their needs.

THE "DIFFICULT" MANAGER

None of us are perfect, and this goes for managers as well as Administrative Assistants. We all have faults, foibles and limitations as well as strengths and good points. Unfortunately, some of us have more negatives than others. So what do you do if you find yourself working for a "difficult" manager? First, you will need to decide if you can live with his/her faults For instance, if he/she is someone who yells at the drop of a paperclip and you come from a family of screamers, you and your manager might get along. On the other hand, if you are someone who cherishes calm and quiet, this might not be a good fit for you. The important point to remember here is we are all unique individuals – what seems like a positive character trait to one person could easily appear to be a character flaw to another – and we all have character flaws! Ideally, the best situation is to work for/with someone whose flaws you can tolerate (and who can tolerate your flaws). However, life is not always ideal and we sometimes have to cope with a less-than-ideal situation. You have several options in this case: you can look for a transfer or a new job; you can stay, get stressed and make yourself sick; you can work to modify the situation; or you can learn to accept it, get on with your work and leave the problems at work. It all depends on how serious the problems are and how well you can handle them.

Perhaps the first thing to do when faced with a difficult manager is to decide what the manager is doing that bothers you. For instance, is your manager always late or a micro-manager, or someone who always gives contradictory and confusing instructions? Is s/he a screamer, a critic, a bully? Then see if you can adjust yourself to the situation –try to develop a work-around or talk to your manager about what is bothering you. S/he might not even be aware that their actions are causing difficulties.

I was in a department where another assistant worked for a manager who was always started the day at least one hour late and this lateness snowballed throughout the day. That assistant got very upset at first; then she got smart – she started building extra time into the schedule, padding travel time and, when that didn't completely solve the problem, the assistant began to gently nag her manager by sending text and email messages at regular intervals (sometimes as often as every 3-5 minutes). Gradually, they both adjusted and the manager was thrilled (and the assistant was able to smile again). It took thoughtful analysis, time and persistence on the part of the Assistant but the problem did become manageable.

Sometimes, the problem can be more difficult. Here are some problems my co-workers and I have had to cope with over the years:

- **Playing favorites** – very hard on the non-favorites who feel abused or neglected, it also creates jealousy between the favorites and non-favorites, which can lead to poor teamwork. If you find yourself in this unfortunate situation you have few options. I would suggest you keep a low profile, do your job and keep see if you can become one of the favorites. If this fails, if might want to see if you can transfer to another department or, if the situation is really difficult, find a job in another company.

- **Micro-management** – managers who do not allow their assistant to think or take the initiative end up with staff who feel frustrated and have little or no sense of accomplishment. Dealing with this situation takes time and patience. I suggest you do the best you can and start slowly to introduce suggestions and modifications. Show your manager that you can be trusted to make small decisions and gradually build up to demonstrate that you are capable of making more and larger decisions. Hopefully, your manager will learn to trust your judgment and will ease off on the micro-management. In the meantime, remain patient and keep making suggestions.

- **Setting unrealistic deadlines** – some managers believe their staff will work better under pressure which leaves their staff stressed, unable to perform proper reviews and proof reading. This can lead to poorly prepared documents for important meetings with both the manager and assistant blaming each other. One way around this situation is to pay attention to your manager's schedule and ask well in advance about what documents will be needed. Try to ease your manager into giving you a little more time by getting the work earlier. If this isn't possible, see if you can start the initial preparation in advance so that you don't have so much to do at the last minute. As with the micro-managers, working this type of manager requires patience and creativity to ease him/her into a more flexible work style.

※ **Personal attacks** - if your manager is attacking you personally, listen to the criticism. If it is about your work, focus on doing your job the way the manager wants you to; perhaps discussing what he/she expects. (It might be better wait until are both calm and have a few free minutes.) If the attacks are personal (your weight, age, or any other "protected" issue), consider talking to someone in your Human Resources Department as this type of behavior is not acceptable (and may not even be legal). Your Human Resources Representative may be able to intervene on your behalf. If you don't get support from your Human Resources representative, consider transferring or getting a different job. No one should have to cope with this type of abuse.

It is easy for me to type "leave, change jobs"; however, I also know that you are the one who will have to make the decision. If you are dealing with a difficult manager, people may tell you to quit but you are the one who will have to find the next job. My advice is to try to line up a new job before you give notice to leave the old one and please do so before the stress on the old job gets so serious that you are get sick – no job is worth your health. If you decide to stay with your current company, here are a few tips for dealing with difficult managers or situations:

- **Do your job well**. Others (including other managers) will notice and you will maintain your self-respect. It will also improve your chances of transferring away from that manager.

- **Pay attention.** Try to figure out what is your manager off; especially if it is an outside influence. For instance, if you notice that s/he comes back angry after meeting with their manager or a particular client, you can be prepared. Stay out of your manager's way to give him/her time to calm down; ask about the meeting to give your manager a chance to vent; or whatever else you think might work.

- **Do your best to keep your own stress levels under control.** Breathe deeply, take a walk, etc. Do not vent to your co-workers but re-read the section in this book on office gossip. If you appear professional and competent in difficult circumstances, you will have a better chance of getting a transfer to a less stressful department.

- **Communicate.** As a last resort, if the stress gets too much, and you want to keep your job, consider talking to your manager. Pick a time when both you and your manager are not overly stressed. Tell him/her how you feel and what you perceive as the problem and, if possible, offer a suggestion or two to improve the situation. It is very important that you keep this non-judgmental and non-accusatory. Do not attack your manager; rather, keep the discussion focused on actions not personalities. Just be prepared – if you take this step and it fails, you might have to consider looking for another job.

Here are a few words of encouragement. I had a difficult manager who was a very controlling micro-manager. I did my best to do my job well; treated my co-workers courteously; provided a helping hand where needed and tried to keep my stress levels under control. Finally, a great position opened up; the manager of that department contacted me and asked if I were interested – I was! My new manager is great; he appreciates my work, gives me projects with reasonable deadlines and the freedom to complete them and is a pleasure to work with.

In conclusion, when I started writing this book, I asked my manager (an amazing boss and terrific person) about his "wish list" for a good assistant. He immediately responded that he needs an assistant with a "sense of humor." He also said that there is nothing worse than starting the day looking at a grumpy assistant. (Many assistants might say the same thing about their managers.) If your manager is a "grump" in the mornings, I suggest you start the ball rolling by greeting him/her each day with a smile; eventually, he/she might respond but at least you will be starting your day off on the right foot.

PERFORMANCE EVALUATIONS

Almost every company has a performance evaluation program. They may have different names for their programs but they all rate or evaluate employees according to a set of standards. These evaluations usually occur at set intervals; you may receive an evaluation as you come off probation for a new position and then, usually, once a year thereafter.

I have seen a few people work very hard to pass their probation evaluation and then sit back and goof off. They haven't lasted long in the company. You should work each day as if you are being evaluated. Don't get paranoid but just do your job to the best of your ability each day. This way, when your evaluation is due, you should pass with good to glowing comments. Additionally, if your company determines merit raises on these evaluations it can be very important incentive to do well on your evaluations.

Some evaluation processes are more complicated than others. At the simplest level, it could just be a printed list of tasks and the manager checks off if you fail, meet, or exceed expectations for each task. At the more complex level, you could be asked to evaluate yourself against a set of standards.

If you find yourself in this situation, be careful. Do not over-rate yourself; rather, try to be realistic. I have been in this type of situation and found it challenging – I gave myself "meet" for almost everything and, fortunately, my manager gave me all "exceeds" for the same list. It is much better to let the manager sing your praises although you shouldn't hide your talents either.

Evaluations have a purpose. They are supposed to show where we need improvement. They can also be a way for you and your manager to evaluate your skills and determine what additional training may be appropriate for you in your current position and as a step toward promotion. If your company and/or manager offer additional training to improve your current skills, or learn new ones, go for it. Company-paid training is a wonderful perk and it looks great on your resume if you want a promotion, transfer, and/or raise.

If your manager takes the time to discuss your evaluation, this could be a good time to bring up some or all of the following points:

- **Extra training**. Either in-house or outside and paid for by the company. Training can be a great way to enhance current skills or to develop new skills. Just make sure the training is related to your job (your manager probably wouldn't approve art classes unless you work in an art department).

- **Tuition reimbursement for college courses**. More and more companies offer this benefit. If it is available, and you have the time, go for it. Getting your company to pay for your college degree is much better than taking on a lot of debt. Just be aware that there may be limits and requirements. In my case, the company I work for offers tuition reimbursement to full time employees after one year of employment. The major also has to be job related and approved by senior management. We also have to maintain at least a "C" average. This still leaves a lot of leeway – I was able to get a degree in business with a computer concentration. I only had to pay for were books and fees. Some companies may restrict which college(s) you can attend; however, many companies are now accepting/approving on-line colleges which are great for people who are self-starters.

- **Special projects.** These can be a great career boost, particularly ones that involve working with other departments. These will help you get noticed and make you and your manager look good.

In conclusion, evaluations are a necessary part of your job. You should make them work to your advantage by doing your best each day and negotiating realistically with your manager. Evaluations do not have to stressful, if you do your job well, you can make your evaluations a positive, rewarding experience.

PROMOTION OPPORTUNITIES

There still seems to a glass ceiling for this type of position; many companies do not promote Administrative Assistants to management positions. However, a good Administrative Assistant can move up to become an Executive Assistant or Office Manager. An Office Manager usually supervises other assistants and clerical support staff while also managing the office. An Executive Assistant will report to a senior member of the company/ This position requires excellent skills and experience and can be very highly paid.

If you have ambitions to move up and out of an assistant position, be sure to discuss this with your manager and/or Human Resources representative. Don't just sit at your desk and wait for a miracle. Ask your manager and/or Human Resources representative about the skills and education required to earn a promotion. Request special assignments to develop and demonstrate your management skills. You might also consider some business or management courses to improve your chances; just check with your Human Resources representative to see if this step would be worthwhile and then check to see if your company will pay for the courses.

You should also look into what type of job openings are occurring and what departments they are in. If possible, get to know some of the people in the department you are targeting. Learn about the department, get to know the manager(s) and build the groundwork in preparation for when you actually do apply for a promotion – this should increase your odds of succeeding. In addition, have periodic meetings with your manager and/or Human Resources representative to discuss your progress; quarterly meetings are usually best.

Over the years, I worked with a number of departments of Administrative Assistants who followed these rules and earned good promotions into management positions. Remember, everyone you meet and/or work with is forming an impression of you – keep your work standards high, your smile cheerful, and your options open. You never know what is awaiting you around the next corner.

ABOUT THE AUTHOR

I have enjoyed working as an Administrative Assistant. This career has been rewarding, interesting and challenging. There have been ups and downs (like any job) but, overall, I am glad I made this choice. While my managers have made the major decisions about my role and assignments, I have had a lot of leeway in how to do the work. I have also had a lot of satisfaction in my career and here are a few examples:

- **Developed** PowerPoint presentations that were used company-wide.

- **Managed** projects that involved multiple buildings in three counties bringing them in on time and under budget with a minimum of disruption to the affected departments and co-workers.

- **Developed** databases to track internal data. In one instance, my manager received a brochure advertising an expensive software package that did what I was already doing; a comparison showed the software in the brochure provided half the features of the one I had created. (I felt great and my managers were suitably impressed).

- **Encouraged** co-workers to apply for transfers and promotions (which they got) and others to go back to college. It is a great feeling to see the people you work with succeed.

- **Made** some great friendships that have stood the test of time as we transferred, got promoted, moved on to other companies or retired. This is probably the best of all.

Whatever you decide to do, I wish you success and hope you have fun along the way.

www.ingramcontent.com/pod-product-compliance
Lightning Source LLC
Chambersburg PA
CBHW061215180526
45170CB00003B/1016